A Parent's Guide to
Critical Race Theory

A Parent's Guide to Critical Race Theory

Fighting CRT in Your Child's School

Christopher Paslay

Contents

Introduction: A Pep Talk for Courageous Parents   7
    Three Truths About Parents Fighting CRT   7
    CRT Litmus Test   8

1 What is Critical Race Theory, Exactly?   11
    Textbook CRT (Theory)   11

2 Critical Race Theory in Practice   17
    CRT in Praxis (Practice)   17

3 Is Critical Race Theory in Your Child's School   31
    Game of Semantics   31
    CRT by Any Other Name   32
    Antiracism   33
    Equity (Or Diversity, Equity, and Inclusion)   34
    Culturally Responsive Teaching   36
    The 1619 Project and 'Accurate History'   38
    Black Lives Matter at School   41
    Red Flags for Concerned Parents   43
    CRT: District vs. Classroom Level   45

4 Identity-Based vs. Principle-Based Approaches   47
    An Identity-Based Approach   48
    A Principle-Based Approach   52
    Principle-Based Educators and Programs   54

5 Resources for Concerned Parents   59
    Organizations Fighting CRT   59
    Toolkits for Challenging CRT   62
    CRT and the Law   64
    Recommended Reading   65
    Books   65
    Articles   65
    A Final Note to Parents   68

About the Author   69

Introduction: A Pep Talk for Courageous Parents

*"It takes a great deal of bravery to stand up to our enemies,
but just as much to stand up to our friends."*

-J.K. Rowling

Thank you parents and community members for taking the time to open this book. This short and concise text, undertaken as a labor of love, is specifically designed to equip mothers, fathers, and concerned citizens with the knowledge, tools, and resources to engage in one of the most important educational battles of our lifetime – the fight against Critical Race Theory infiltrating K-12 schools. Although these materials center on American education, the pushback against CRT has become global, and as such, these resources can be extended and applied to classrooms and school districts around the world.

Three Truths About Parents Fighting CRT

To the parents fighting against CRT: *You are not racist or bad people.* Your instincts about Critical Race Theory are correct, and that feeling in your gut – the one that says something just isn't right in your child's school – is authentic and real. Something *isn't* right in K-12 education today, and more and more parents are waking up to this reality every day.

To the parents fighting against CRT: *You are not alone.* The majority of Americans oppose CRT.[1] You may have been told otherwise, by another parent or teacher or school board member who insists you are ignorant or misinformed, that you are simply a member of some fringe group getting in the way of progress, but they have it *backwards.* You are part of a steadily growing movement of concerned parents across America, mothers and fathers of all races and political affiliations, who know in their hearts CRT is the wrong way to go.

---

[1] In June of 2021, The Economist/YouGov released a poll that showed 58 percent of Americans found the controversial curriculum somewhat or very unfavorable. Only 38 percent said they viewed Critical Race Theory favorably.

To the parents fighting against CRT: *You are on the right side of history.* The pushback against CRT is an organic extension of the Civil Rights Movement, and falls directly in line with Dr. Martin Luther King Jr.'s "Dream." Those pushing CRT, who now teach that color-blindness is "racist," are the ones who have lost their way. History will expose their cynicism, polarization, and vindictiveness, and reveal that using an identity-based approach focusing on skin color – as opposed to a principle-based approach focusing on the content of character – was wrong-headed and counterproductive.

CRT Litmus Test

Before you read any further, ask yourself these **10 questions**:

1. Should we be teaching children that all White people are inherently racist? This is a central point made by Robin DiAngelo, who makes top dollar facilitating professional development trainings for teachers and other organizations. Her bestselling book, *White Fragility*, has been used to develop so-called "antiracist" curriculum in school districts all across America.

2. Should we be teaching children that America is a systemically racist country based in White supremacy? The Oregon Department of Education is promoting a program called "A Pathway to Equitable Math Instruction," which aims to deconstruct racism in mathematics, and make visible the "toxic characteristics of White supremacy culture in math."

3. Should we be teaching children that all racial disparities are the sole result of racism? Ibram X. Kendi, who runs the Center for Antiracist Research at Boston University, forwards this very idea. He's proposed passing an antiracist constitutional amendment to "fix the original sin of racism" in America. This amendment would not be concerned with equal opportunity, but equal outcome, and any racial disparity would be viewed as the result of racist policy and would be adjusted accordingly.

4. Should we be teaching children that you are either racist or antiracist, and that there is no neutral? Kendi's bestselling book, *How to Be an Antiracist*, polarizes Americans into separate camps and presents educators with the fallacy of the false dilemma: you either accept Kendi's polarizing ideology wholeheartedly, or risk getting labeled "racist."

5. Should we be teaching children that White America is inherently anti-Black, and that all Whites suffer from an unconscious bias against people of color? Seattle Public Schools held a teacher training where educators were found guilty of "spirit murder," which is the concept that American schools "murder the souls of Black children every day through systemic, institutionalized, anti-Black, state-sanctioned violence," according to University of Georgia education professor Bettina Love.

6. Should we be polarizing children into tribal camps based on race, and teaching them to view the world as oppressors vs. oppressed? According to a study by The Heritage Foundation, a major thematic component of Critical Race Theory is the "Marxist analysis of society made up of categories of oppressors and oppressed."

7. Should we be teaching children that things such as linear time, work ethic, individualism, and the scientific method are aspects of White supremacy culture? In July of 2020, the National Museum of African American History and Culture published a pamphlet titled "Aspects and Assumptions of Whiteness in the United States" which did just that.

8. Should we be teaching children that so-called "Whiteness" is problematic, and must be targeted and disrupted? An organization of English teachers called "Disrupt Texts" wants to remove White authors like William Shakespeare from English classes, and Bree Picower, an education professor at Montclair State University in New Jersey, published a book titled *Reading Writing and Racism: Disrupting Whiteness in Teacher Education and in the Classroom*, which teaches education majors that so-called "Whiteness" is something that must be eliminated in classrooms.

9. Should we be teaching children that being nice, cooperative, and compliant is racist, and that White silence is violence? In July of 2020, KIPP charter school founder Richard Barth announced KIPP was retiring its national slogan, "Work hard. Be nice." According to Barth, the slogan "ignores the significant effort required to dismantle systemic racism, places value on being compliant and submissive, supports the illusion of meritocracy, and does not align with our vision of students being free to create the future they want."

10. Should we be teaching children that the most important determinant of success in their lives is skin color? Critical Race Theory, and all of its instructional offshoots, teaches a concept called "race-consciousness," which racializes all aspects of society and makes skin color the primary lens from which children are taught to view the world.

If you answered *no* to any of these questions, and feel in your gut that CRT is wrongheaded and counterproductive, please continue reading this book. The book's ultimate mission – in addition to helping parents win the battle against CRT in K-12 classrooms – is to bring all people together, to celebrate our differences but *move past them* to the things that bond us as human beings; tragically, our very mission of finding universal human bonds directly contradicts the fundamental teachings of CRT, which argue such things as common values are not possible.

To win the battle against CRT, however, parents must understand what they are up against, and learn to expose and challenge CRT where it exists. This book presents a three-step process to do just that: **understand, expose, and challenge CRT**.

The first two chapters of this book help parents **understand** what CRT is exactly, from its theoretical tenets as they developed in academia (Chapter One), to the ways in which CRT directly manifests in K-12 classrooms (Chapter Two).

Chapter Three gives parents practical information and techniques to **expose** CRT in their own K-12 schools, and helps them sift through constantly changing definitions in an effort to help them navigate semantics and deal with the language games often played by school boards and CRT advocates.

Chapter Four helps parents **challenge** CRT in their own school districts, providing sound alternatives that use core principles and values instead of identity to drive quality instruction for all children.

Finally, Chapter Five offers a collection of **practical resources** for parents to use in their fight against CRT, which include information on parent groups and toolkits, links to freedom of information forms and documents, recommended readings, and examples of curriculum and training that violate students' and teachers' rights, which can lead to possible legal action.

Unlike the use of critical pedagogy stemming from CRT ("pedagogy" is a big word for "teaching strategy"), which is cynically designed for *disruption and resistance* and little else, this book offers solutions. It adopts a principle-based approach rooted in shared educational and personal values on an *individual level*, which is the key to equality and justice.

Chapter One: What Is Critical Race Theory, Exactly?

"[C]ritical race theory questions the very foundations of the liberal order, including equality theory, legal reasoning, Enlightenment rationalism, and neutral principle of constitutional law.

-Richard Delgado & Jean Stefancic

Critical Race Theory, or CRT, is not new. It's been around since the late 1970s, although its use was mostly confined to legal scholars and academics inside colleges and universities. As CRT and the ideas surrounding it have developed over the past 40 years, it can now be viewed in terms of theory (theoretical tenets in journals and textbooks) and praxis (application of CRT in society, including K-12 schools).

Textbook CRT (Theory)

Textbook CRT is quite radical, and its advocates openly admit they *do not* continue the legacy of the Civil Rights Movement.[2] In the book, *Critical Race Theory: The Key Writings That Formed the Movement*, co-authored by leading CRT legal scholar Kimberle Crenshaw, it states "The aspect of our work which most markedly distinguishes it from conventional liberal and conservative legal scholarship about race and inequality is a deep dissatisfaction with traditional civil rights discourse."[3]

In other words, critical race theorists wanted to break away from the traditional values of the Civil Rights Movement, because they argued that these ideals were not bringing racial progress fast enough, or were perpetuating the same racial inequality as before.

---

[2] This section is adapted from Ryan Chapman's "A Guide To Critical Race Theory," which can be accessed at https://www.youtube.com/watch?v=2rDu_VUpoJ8&t=381s

[3] *Critical Race Theory: The Key Writings That Formed the Movement*, by Kimberle Crenshaw, Neil Gotanda, Gary Peller, & Kendell Thomas, 1996

One traditional civil rights value critical race theorists opposed was the notion of "color-blindness," which can be encompassed in MLK's "I Have A Dream" speech, where he stated he hoped for a time when his four little children "will one day live in a nation where they will not be judged by the color of their skin but by the content of their character."

But those frustrated with the Civil Rights Movement of the 1950s and 1960s did not believe color-blindness was attainable, as they cynically claimed it was impossible *not* to see color. In fact, those pushing CRT insisted color-blindness was in many cases a ruse, because racism was still taking place throughout society, despite this so-called "color-blindness" push by people like MLK.

As stated in *Critical Race Theory: The Key Writings That Formed the Movement*, "The belief in color-blindness and equal process, however, would make no sense at all in a society in which identifiable groups had actually been treated differently historically and in which the effects of this difference in treatment continued into the present."[4]

Instead of standing firm to MLK's "Dream" and doubling efforts to get past race and come to a place of deeper understanding, critical race theorists gave up on the concept altogether, and rejected the notion that people could ever connect through universal values, or that America could ever live up to its founding principles because they came from a White supremacist (White dominant) society.

Thus, the goal of CRT was not to *improve* society, but to *remake or transform it*. In essence, critical race theorists believed the bulk of America's values, systems, culture, traditions, norms, etc. had to be uprooted and disrupted, as they inherently privileged Whites and sought to oppress people of color.

A second traditional value from the Civil Rights Movement that critical race theorists disagreed with was racial integration. Racial integration was the idea that it was possible for people of all identity groups to come together and bond through mutually agreed upon values – core principles that would allow *all people* to share societal resources and political power equally.

---

[4] *Critical Race Theory: The Key Writings That Formed the Movement*

But advocates of CRT believed that finding so-called "shared" or "mutually agreed upon" values was impossible, because societal power hierarchies – which favored Whites – would make these values biased against people of color. Therefore, they cynically believed the notion of integration was false and misleading, as universal values were simply "White values," which continued to keep resources and political power from people of color.

Simply put, Whites and Blacks coming together through a common culture was not possible, because Whites ultimately controlled this culture, and used it to keep power and resources for themselves.

In fact, CRT proponents argued that civil rights activists were allowing the dominant majority group (Whites) to effectively destroy the culture and identity of minority groups (people of color) through a process called "cultural genocide," also referred to as "assimilation" or "White acculturalization."[5]

This is where the culture of the dominant group takes over the cultures of smaller groups, forcing these groups to drop their own culture and adopt the culture of the dominant group. The solution to this, according to proponents of CRT, was "race-consciousness," which was a hyper-focus on race, identity, and culture. In other words, all things in society should be racialized, and viewed through the lens of race and skin color – so the cultures of marginalized groups could be watched and protected.

To push back against so-called White "assimilation" or White dominant culture, critical race theorists called for Black liberation, which resisted America as a "melting pot" with a national cultural identity, and insisted so-called "oppressed" cultures should actively promote and assert their own cultures and identities as part of the struggle toward freedom.

In other words, marginalized groups must fight back against having their own culture taken from them by actively promoting their cultural identities, and by refusing to "blend in" with a shared national culture. The teachings of Malcolm X., who was a Black separatist raised on the writings of Marcus Garvey (also a Black separatist), are often used by advocates of CRT, who feel oppressed cultures can (and should) live as independent, culturally distinct entities within America.[6]

---

[5] "A Critique of 'Our Constitution Is Color-Blind,'" by Neil Gotanda, *Stanford Law Review*, November, 1991

[6] "Race Consciousness," Gary Peller, *Duke Law Review*, 1990

CRT advocates wanted to use race-consciousness to analyze and understand America in a new way. Specifically, they used something called "deconstruction" to make new observations about the way race and racism impacted American society and life.[7]

Deconstruction is when you take something apart, piece by piece, in order to analyze it so you can put it back together again in a new way. Critical race theorists wanted to use deconstruction to break down all of America's systems into smaller parts, and see how race and identity operated within these systems.

According to CRT scholars Richard Delgado and Jean Stefancic, critical race theorists wanted to "question the very foundations of the liberal order, including equality theory, legal reasoning, Enlightenment rationalism, and neutral principle of constitutional law."[8]

In other words, CRT proponents wanted to use deconstruction at every level of society, taking apart things like American law, government, and education - questioning the very meanings of words within our language – in order to break these things up and make them easier to change.

Once America's systems were successfully taken apart, critical race theorists wanted to "reconstruct" America and make everyone race-conscious, and to convince society that the civil rights values of color-blindness and integration were not only impossible, but were an attempt to destroy the cultures of smaller groups and to replace them with White culture.

To stop such White oppressiveness, Americans should be eternally race-conscious, never stop challenging inherently racist American systems, and work to spread the principles of CRT through continuous lobbying, organizing, and social justice activism – known today as "doing the work."

---

[7] "Race, Reform, and Retrenchment: Transformation and Legitimation in Antidiscrimination Law," by Kimberle Williams Crenshaw, *Harvard Law Review*, September 10, 2020

[8] *Critical Race Theory: An Introduction*, by Richard Delgado & Jean Stefancic, March, 2017

Originally, CRT stayed within the walls of higher education, and up until recently, existed mostly in colleges and universities. It was here that CRT started to deconstruct (break down in order to reassemble) universal principles of academic scholarship – things like objectivity, neutrality, and balance. These principles were eventually reconstructed and deemed aspects of so-called "White culture," and were no longer considered the shared values of America or the academic world.

As such, scholars and academics strived for "authenticity," which resisted integration into "White culture," and moved away from objectivity, neutrality, and balance to works that were "authentic," or of being "true to oneself and one's world."[9] In other words, truth became subjective and was based on "lived experience," and the cultural perspectives of the scholars completing the work.

According to *Words That Wound: Critical Race Theory, Assaultive Speech, And The First Amendment*, "Critical race theorists embrace subjectivity of perspective and are avowedly political."[10] So in addition to rejecting color-blindness and an integration of shared culture and values, CRT proponents rejected the idea that academics should be neutral and free from politics. Put another way, they argued that "truth" was subjective and consciously injected a political agenda into their work.

Critical Race Theory stemmed from an earlier school of thought called "Critical Theory," the development of which is credited in large part to German philosopher Max Horkheimer of the Frankfurt School of social research (which was anti-capitalist). Horkheimer believed critical theorists should work in academia not to find objective truth, but to forward their political goals. As such, they should purposefully slant their research and findings to accommodate their politics, which in part was aimed at ending so-called "oppression."[11]

---

[9] "Critical Race Theory, Archie Shepp, and Fire Music: Securing an Authentic Intellectual Life in a Multicultural World," by John O. Calmore, *California Law Review*, 1992

[10] *Words That Wound: Critical Race Theory, Assaultive Speech, And The First Amendment*, by Mari J. Matsuda, Charles R. Lawrence, Richard Delgado, & Kimberle Crenshaw, 1993

[11] *Critical Theory: Selected Essays*, by Max Horkheimer, 1972

Critical Theory also incorporated elements of Marxism, which attempted to bring resistance and political activism through awareness of suffering at the hands of a power hierarchy (oppressors vs. oppressed). It sought to exploit the anger the poor felt for the rich, and then use this anger to organize, protest, and revolt against the status quo. Only critical theorists replaced class struggle (rich vs. poor) with identity (Black vs. White, male vs. female, gay vs. straight, etc.).

This is a broad (and hopefully understandable) roadmap of the fundamental development and ideas at the heart of Critical Race Theory. Now that the textbook theory has been laid out, the praxis (the application of these approaches) can be better studied, particularly in K-12 schools across America.

Chapter Two: Critical Race Theory in Practice

"Critical Race Theory reformulates the old Marxist dichotomy
of oppressor and oppressed, replacing the class categories of bourgeoisie and
proletariat with the identity categories of White and Black."

-Christopher Rufo

Critical Race Theory has permeated all levels of American society. Its concepts have long left academia and are now found in training manuals in government agencies, in H.R. departments of major corporations, in the United States military, and most concerning, in K-12 classrooms across America (as well as many European countries).

CRT in Praxis (Practice)

To trace the insidious growth of CRT in our children's schools, a clear and concise summary of its main principles are needed. They are as follows:

- **Color-consciousness**. CRT rejects traditional color-blindness in favor of a racialized worldview which sees all aspects of society through the lens of skin color. All systems in America, at all levels of society, must be analyzed through race. This is a formal rejection of MLK's "content of character," a major ideal of the Civil Rights Movement.

- **Cultural separatism**. CRT rejects the concept of universal values and a shared American culture, which CRT insists are not possible because White supremacy (White culture) dominates society As such, non-White groups must collectively fight for the continual promotion of their own cultures and values. This is a formal rejection of integration, a second major ideal of the Civil Rights Movement.

- **Opposition to Whiteness**. Because CRT rejects integration and pushes the continual promotion of smaller group values, Whiteness (White Dominance) must be challenged and disrupted in order to stop cultural genocide and White acculturalization (non-White groups assimilating into the dominant culture).

- **Emphasis on systems**. CRT emphasizes systems over individuals, and believes so-called "oppression" can only be adequately solved through systemic change, and that the effectiveness of individualism and meritocracy is limited. In short, oppressive systems will ultimately negate hard work, and the notion of "personal responsibility" is false and misleading.

- **Use of Marxism**. CRT attempts to bring resistance and political activism through awareness of suffering at the hands of a power hierarchy (oppressors vs. oppressed), and attempts to use the anger of so-called marginalized groups to organize, protest, and revolt against the status quo.

- **Use of deconstruction**. CRT uses "deconstruction," the process of breaking things down into smaller parts in order to rebuild them, to remake traditional American systems, culture, values, language, etc. according to the principles of CRT.

- **Subjective truth**. CRT denies the existence of objective truth, and believes objectivity, neutrality, and balance are "White" values. It teaches truth is subjective, changes according to culture, and is the result of lived experience.

- **Political activism**. CRT's end goal is always political activism – "doing the work." Its proponents are involved in the continuous struggle to push CRT ideology through sustained advocacy, lobbying, and protest.

Now that these principles have been laid bare, it becomes possible to trace CRT through K-12 education.

First, CRT is infiltrating American education through color-consciousness. K-12 education, like all aspects of American society, has become acutely racialized. R.I. Meyerholz Elementary School in Cupertino, California, forced third-graders to deconstruct their racial identities, then rank themselves according to their "power and privilege." They also separated the eight-year-old children into oppressors and oppressed.[12]

---

[12] "Woke Elementary," by Christopher Rufo, *City Journal*, January 13, 2021

In March of 2021, the Arizona Department of Education created educational "equity" resources claiming that babies show the first signs of racism at three months old and that White children "remain strongly biased in favor of Whiteness" by age five. As reported in *City Journal*, "The Department of Education recommends a reading that claims babies are not 'colorblind' and that parents must instill 'antiracist attitudes and actions' beginning at birth, in order for their children to not 'absorb bias from the world around them.'"[13]

Tragically, this emphasis on "color-consciousness" is directly impacting instruction and discipline in K-12 schools across America. The teaching of rigorous academic skills are now being implemented not according to interest or ability level, but according to race. Entire academic courses in schools are being cancelled because racial quotas – as determined through "equity audits" – are not being met. Honors and A.P. classes are getting scrapped and eliminated because they are seen as "too White."[14]

Likewise, racial quota systems are being used to implement discipline. Many schools no longer look at behavior as a measure for discipline, but skin color. Following the lead of the Obama administration's 2014 "Dear Colleague" letter – which issued guidance to public schools aimed at making discipline rates proportionate across all races – schools stopped traditional discipline measures as not to draw the wrath of the U.S. Department of Education and lose federal funding.

The result? Learning environments across the nation were compromised, harming the educations of thousands of students, many of whom were children of color.[15]

CRT is infiltrating American education through cultural separatism. Tragically, too many K-12 schools have abandoned the idea that there are universal principles and values that connect us all as human beings, or that there exist fundamental skills for success that transcend race and identity. Books like *The 7 Habits of Highly Effective Teens* are being replaced with Ibram X. Kendi's *How To Be An Antiracist*, which literally separates kids into two groups, "racists" and "antiracists."

---

[13] "Racism in the Cradle," by Christopher Rufo, christopherrufo.com, March 2, 2021

[14] "To Address Inequity, Let's Do More Than Eliminate 'Gifted And Talented' Programs," Natalie Wexler, *Forbes*, August 28, 2019

[15] "Discipline Reform Through the Eyes of Teachers," David Griffith and Adam Tyner, Fordham Institute, July 2019

If a child agrees with Kendi's ideology, he or she is considered to be part of the progress, and is an "antiracist." But if the child is not committed to the whole antiracist paradigm (or has an alternative perspective or solution), he or she is a "racist," as there is no neutral.[16] Although the term "antiracist" sounds well meaning, the concept is complex and in certain cases uses discrimination to end discrimination, as will be discussed in Chapter Three.

In October of 2020, at the King County Library System in Seattle, a private consulting firm called Racial Equity Consultants held racially segregated "listening sessions," where Whites and people of color were separated in different rooms and were lectured on systemic racism and antiracism.[17] Known as "affinity groups" or racial "caucusing," these approaches come from a place of clear separation as opposed to cooperation.

What were once considered universal skills for achievement and academic success have now been rebranded as values of White people only. In July of 2020, the Smithsonian's National Museum of African American History and Culture published a pamphlet called "Aspects and Assumptions of Whiteness and White Culture in the United States," which stated that things like hard work, self-reliance, a two-parent nuclear family, objectivity, rational linear thinking, ridged time schedules, competition, politeness, and the written word were not universal values that students should aspire to, but were elements of White supremacy culture.

In March of 2021, the California Department of Education adopted its "Ethnic Studies Model Curriculum" for K-12 schools. An educator named R. Tolteka Cuauhtin developed much of the material regarding early American history. In his book *Rethinking Ethnic Studies*, which is cited throughout the curriculum, Cuauhtin argues that the United States was founded on a "Eurocentric, White supremacist (racist, anti-Black, anti-Indigenous), capitalist (classist), patriarchal (sexist and misogynistic), heteropatriarchal (homophobic), and anthropocentric paradigm brought from Europe."[18]

---

[16] *How To Be An Antiracist*, by Ibram X. Kendi, August, 2019

[17] "The New Segregation," Christopher Rufo, *City Journal*, October 19, 2020

[18] "Revenge of the Gods," Christopher Rufo, *City Journal*, March 10, 2021

In other words, America's founding principles and values as conceived in the Declaration of Independence and Constitution were not universal truths that were self-evident, but oppressive White supremacy.

Educators at The Daulton School, a prestigious private school located on the Upper East Side of Manhattan, seemed to believe as much. In December of 2020, dozens of Daulton faculty members signed a controversial 8-page antiracist manifesto with multiple demands, some of which included requiring courses that focus on "Black liberation" and "challenges to White supremacy," overhauling Daulton's entire curriculum to make it more diverse, and requiring antiracism statements from all staffers, among other demands.[19]

CRT is infiltrating American education through opposition to Whiteness. In February of 2020, North Carolina's largest school district launched a campaign against "Whiteness in educational spaces" – and trained teachers to push the ideology of "antiracism" directly onto students without parental permission. According to an article in *City Journal*:

> At the first session, "Whiteness in Ed Spaces," school administrators provided two handouts on the "norms of Whiteness." These documents claimed that "(White) cultural values" include "denial," "fear," "blame," "control," "punishment," "scarcity," and "one-dimensional thinking." According to notes from the session, the teachers argued that "Whiteness perpetuates the system" of injustice and that the district's "whitewashed curriculum" was "doing real harm to our students and educators." The group encouraged White teachers to "challenge the dominant ideology" of Whiteness and "disrupt" White culture in the classroom through a series of "transformational interventions."[20]

In February of 2021, New York's East Side Community School sent a letter encouraging White parents to become "White traitors" and advocate for "White abolition." According to *City Journal*:

---

[19] Uproar at NYC's posh Dalton School after faculty issues 8-page anti-racism manifesto," by Susan Edelman & Dana Kennedy, *New York Post*, December 19, 2020

[20] "Subversive Education," by Christopher Rufo, *City Journal*, March 17, 2021

The message, sent by principal Mark Federman, showed a graphic outlining eight stages of White identity development—from the lowest form, "White supremacist," to the intermediate forms of "White confessional" and "White traitor," to the highest form, "White abolitionist." The goal of this process, according to the graphic's creator, Northwestern University professor Barnor Hesse, is to challenge the "regime of Whiteness" and eventually to "subvert White authority" and "not [allow] Whiteness to reassert itself."[21]

In February of 2021, Bree Picower, an education professor at Montclair State University, published a book titled, *Reading, Writing, and Racism: Disrupting Whiteness in Teacher Education and in the Classroom.* This book is aimed at college education majors and student-teachers, and teaches that so-called "Whiteness" is something that must be targeted and eliminated in schools, classrooms, and curriculum.

In June of 2020, Anastasia Higginbotham wrote a children's picture book titled, *Not My Idea: A Book About Whiteness,* which teaches young kids that "Whiteness is a bad deal," and suggests it's evil and associated with the devil. This book has been used in a number of kindergarten and elementary schools across the nation.

A group of K-12 educators, headed by a Pennsylvania ELA teacher named Tricia Ebarvia, have formed a group called "Disrupt Texts," which aims to remove White literature (including Shakespeare) from English classes by racializing the universal themes found in classic literature.

The opposition to Whiteness in K-12 schools is steadily growing. An increasing number of educators, who espouse the insidious principles at the heart of CRT, are perpetuating the notion that Whiteness is something that must be targeted, disrupted, and eliminated.

CRT is infiltrating American education through the emphasis on systems. Tragically, the ideals of self-reliance, individualism, and personal responsibility are under attack in the United States. While there are many factors that influence a student's achievement in school and success in life, CRT has effectively nullified change on a personal level and shifted the focus to systems. So-called "systemic racism" is now seen as the root of all racial disparities in the United States.

---

[21] "Gone Crazy," by Christopher Rufo, *City Journal*, February 18, 2021

As such, a major goal in K-12 schools is to end "White privilege" and "White supremacy," and to put a stop to systemic injustice. Notions of self-reliance, individualism, and personal responsibility are not only discounted and discredited, but are even viewed as racist examples of White supremacy culture.

Last year, Portland Public Schools trained children to become race-conscious revolutionaries by teaching that racism "infects the very structure(s) of our society."[22] In Tigard, Oregon, a suburb southwest of Portland, the Tigard-Tualatin School District created a "Department of Equity and Inclusion" to end such systemic injustice, and installed social-justice activist Zinnia Un as director.

As reported in *City Journal*:

> In her blueprint, Un describes the new oppressor as an amalgamation of "Whiteness," "colorblindness," "individualism," and "meritocracy." These are the values of capitalist society — but for Un, they are the values of *White* society, the primary impediment to social justice.[23]

In January of 2021, Christopher Rufo reported that San Diego Public Schools accused White teachers of being colonizers on stolen Native American land and told them "you are racist" and "you are upholding racist ideas, structures, and policies."

As Rufo reported:

> Nonetheless, the "antiracism" narrative has tremendous momentum in modern educational institutions. It reduces complex phenomena to a simple explanation of White racism – and lets teachers of all racial backgrounds shift blame for failing schools to the abstract forces of "systemic oppression." Eventually, however, there will be a price. School districts such as San Diego Unified can spend millions on trainings, speeches, and diversity audits, but none of these efforts is likely to result in better academic results.[24]

---

[22] "The Child Soldiers of Portland," Christopher Rufo, *City Journal*, Spring, 2021

[23] "The Child Soldiers of Portland," Christopher Rufo

[24] "Radicals in the Classroom," Christopher Rufo, *City Journal*, January 5, 2021

CRT is infiltrating American education through the use of Marxism. Karl Marx attempted to bring resistance and political activism through awareness of suffering at the hands of a power hierarchy, pitting the impoverished proletariat (workers) against the bourgeoise (capitalist owners).

This oppressor vs. oppressed dynamic (further developed by Marxist Brazilian educator Paulo Freire's *Pedagogy of the Oppressed*), has been co-opted by critical race theorists and used in K-12 schools. However, *social class* has been replaced with *race and identity,* and instead of rich vs. poor, it's now White vs. Black, male vs. female, straight vs. gay, Christian vs. Muslim, etc.

At Cherokee Middle School in Springfield, Missouri, teachers were required to locate themselves on an "oppression matrix," and were told that White heterosexual Protestant males were inherently oppressors and had to atone for their "covert White supremacy."[25]

At the elite United Nations International School in New York City, students launched an anonymous social-media campaign denouncing their teachers and administrators for their "vast history of systemic racism," "White-liberal racist thinking" and "direct, intentional, repeated racial trauma." The students threatened to "cancel" their "oppressors" through social-media shaming – and administrators immediately caved in to their demands.

As reported in the *New York Post*:

> The saga began last June, when a group of students launched an anonymous Instagram channel, Black at UNIS, where they posted dozens of anonymous and unverified accusations against the school and specific teachers. The accusations range from "micro-aggressions" — a teacher who "used to mix up names of Black students" — to "White leadership failure," such as allegedly refusing to hire Black teachers and ignoring the bullying of Black students.[26]

---

[25] "'Antiracism'" Comes to the Heartland," Christopher Rufo, *City Journal*, January 19, 2021

[26] "Manhattan's most privileged kids play victim — and their teachers cave," by Christopher Rufo, *New York Post*

A common theme underlying K-12 education today is that White teachers are privileged "oppressors" who must unpack their internalized racial superiority, while students of color are victims who must root out their internalized "oppression."

CRT is infiltrating American education through the use of deconstruction. As the saying goes, he who defines the terms, controls the argument. Educators pushing CRT have successfully redefined much of the language surrounding race and racism by deconstructing concepts and terms, and then reconstructing them to mean something totally different. Likewise, many words and phrases have been deemed "politically incorrect" and have been summarily replaced, literally overnight.

Antiracist educator and critical Whiteness scholar Robin DiAngelo, whose book *White Fragility* has sold over a million copies, has helped redefine such terms as "racist" and "racism" (which now inherently apply to *all* Whites, regardless of actual prejudice or discrimination), as well as "Whiteness" and "White supremacy" (which now inherently applies to all aspects of American society that is majority European-American).[27]

New words, phrases, and concepts – like "anti-Blackness," "intersectionality," "equity," and "antiracism" – come into existence through critical race theorists in academia, and these concepts soon take hold. Tragically, most of mainstream society has no understanding of such ideas, or worse, *misunderstands* them.

Eventually, as the language is redefined through CRT manipulation and political correctness, the culture of America is changed. Traditional customs, values, and ideals are suddenly out of fashion, or are viewed as archaic or even "racist" – not because they are discriminatory or intolerant, but because they've been *redefined to be so.*

The rewriting of Martin Luther King Jr.'s "Dream," along with the notion of traditional colorblindness, is perhaps the most tragic example of deconstruction. Dr. King rightfully believed in the classic liberal idea of judging a person not by the color of their skin, but by the content of their character. In other words, he preached that we must acknowledge and celebrate our differences, but *move past them* to a deeper place of human connection.

---

[27] *What Does It Mean To Be White?: Developing White Racial Literacy*, by Robin DiAngelo

However, CRT advocates have hijacked traditional colorblindness and repackaged it as "color-blind racism," falsely claiming that to be "color-blind" means to refuse to see color, and by default, refuse to see racism and racial injustice.

Deconstruction is often times disingenuous, as it purposely redefines opposing positions in a way that cripples them, and makes them easier to nullify or dismiss.

Deconstruction can become Orwellian, as it attempts to literally control the words we can and can't say, which leads to policing thoughts – ideas we can and can't *think*.

In March of 2021 Grace Church School, an elite prep school in downtown Manhattan, published a 12-page memo that encouraged people to stop using certain terms that it considered to be outdated, and to replace those terms with "inclusive" terminology. The new terms were billed as "neutral," however they were anything but, as they *replaced* words that were deemed politically incorrect. The "inclusive" terminology was actually *exclusive*, as it attempted to weed out words and phrases contrary to the worldviews of the administration.

Some examples were:

- Instead of saying, "mom and dad," say, "grown-ups," "folks," "or family."
- Instead of saying, "parents," say, "grown-ups," "folks," "family," "and guardians."
- Instead of saying, "Merry Christmas!/Happy Holidays!" say, "Have a great break!"
- Instead of saying, "diverse/minority," say, "person of color, marginalized identity/population."

The memo also redefined these terms:

- **Colorblind** – No one is color blind as it pertains to race. We see the skin tones of people and assumptions are made about how someone identifies racially.
- **Caucasian** – The correct term is White. White is a more accurate description of light-skinned people of European descent.

- **Traditional Family**—We actively try to undo notions of a "typical" or "normal" family structure, each family is unique.[28]

CRT is infiltrating American education through the idea of subjective truth. According to critical race theorists, there is no objective "truth," only a subjective reality based on lived experience. CRT doesn't view *perception of truth* as subjective (which would indeed be based on lived experience), but sees *truth itself* as subjective. This becomes problematic in K-12 education, as much of the state standards and content being taught is indeed objective information that *isn't* based on lived experience, especially in math and science.

But this hasn't stopped CRT from infiltrating math and science in K-12 schools across America. In 2019, in an effort to push "culturally responsive pedagogy," the Seattle school district began promoting ethnocentric math via their "K-12 Math Ethnic Studies Framework," where learning objectives included asking questions like: *What is my mathematical identity? Who gets to say if an answer is right? How has math been used to resist and liberate people and communities of color from oppression? When do I know/feel like I am a mathematician? Can you advocate against oppressive mathematical practices?*[29]

In the winter of 2021, the Oregon Department of Education began promoting a program called "A Pathway to Equitable Math Instruction," which aimed to deconstruct racism in mathematics, and make visible the "toxic characteristics of White supremacy culture in math."

During the 2020-21 school year, the Illinois State Board of Education approved a resolution to incorporate "Culturally Responsive Teaching and Leading" standards into Illinois K-12 schools. These standards watered down instructional rigor and undermined the concept of objective truth. One of the standards read, "Understand and value . . . that there is not one 'correct' way of doing or understanding something, and that what is seen as 'correct' is most often based on our lived experiences."[30]

---

[28] "NYC School Pushes Students To Stop Saying 'Mom,' 'Dad,' 'Parents,' Referring To People By Gender," by Ryan Saavedra, *New York Post*, March 11, 2021

[29] "In Seattle, math is cultural appropriation," by Madeline Fry Schultz, *Washington Examiner*, October 23, 2019

[30] Illinois State Board of Education Notice of Proposed Amendments, https://www.thomasmoresociety.org/wp-content/uploads/2020/11/Proposed-Reguations-to-ISBE-from-register_volume44_issue_37.pdf

CRT is infiltrating American education through political activism. One of CRT's biggest end goals is the forwarding of its ideology through activism. The notion that "teaching is a political act," along with the push by social justice advocates to embed the "struggle against oppression" into lessons and activities, has helped politics supersede academic instruction.

Political activist groups, like Black Lives Matter, are now writing curriculum for K-12 schools, and America's biggest teachers union have gotten on board; the National Education Association formally adopted using BLM curriculum in its schools in a business resolution in 2017.

Activists groups regularly write "teacher resources" that make it into K-12 schools, often times through the backdoor. Philadelphia's Racial Justice Organizing is one group. An activist group called "Mikva Challenge" out of Chicago is another. There are literally dozens of them all across the United States, non-profits or other social justice outfits writing CRT-based curriculum with a clear political agenda that regularly ends up in K-12 schools, circumventing school boards and state legislatures.

So-called "racial," "equity," or "diversity" consulting firms – like Glenn Singleton's Courageous Conversations – also usher in the use of identity politics.[31] One of Singleton's activities is called "The Color Line," which requires teachers to answer 25 questions about their race and privilege, add up their scores, and then line-up in the room according to their scores – paying close attention to the scores of those around them.

Corwin Press's math textbook titled, *High School Mathematics Lessons to Explore, Understand, and Respond to Social Injustice,* literally indoctrinates students to think certain ways about controversial issues (like systemic racism, minimum wage, immigration, and border security), and offers lessons and activities that promote social protests and rallies.

In 2021, the Santa Clara County Office of Education denounced the United States as a "parasitic system" based on the "invasion" of "White male settlers" and encouraged teachers to "cash in on kids' inherent empathy" in order to recruit them into political activism.

As reported by Christopher Rufo:

---

[31] *Courageous Conversations About Race,* by Glenn E. Singleton, 2005

Earlier this year, the state Department of Education approved an ethnic studies model curriculum, and individual school districts have begun to implement programs that advocate "decolonizing" the United States and "liberating" students from capitalism, patriarchy, and settler colonialism.[32]

Perhaps the most concerning trend regarding the infiltration of political activism into K-12 schools is something called "action civics." In a report by Stanley Kurtz titled, "'Action Civics' Replaces Citizenship with Partisanship," the insidious nature of CRT's influence on policy becomes clear. Kurtz writes:

> Unfortunately, widespread adoption of Action Civics will definitively politicize an already politically tainted K-12 educational system, irrevocably cementing the partisan Left's hold upon our culture. Action civics amounts to school-sponsored indoctrination and political action in support of progressive policy positions. It must be energetically opposed by all who value authentic liberal education. . . .

> Action Civics conceives of itself as a living laboratory in which mere civic theory is put productively into practice. Students, it is held, best acquire civic know-how through direct political action, for example by protesting in favor of gun control or lobbying for legislation to address climate change.[33]

In other words, action civics could offer class credit for political protest – a clear violation of educational ethics.

By tracing Critical Race Theory's main principles – **color-consciousness, cultural separatism, opposition to Whiteness, emphasis on systems, use of Marxism, use of deconstruction, subjective truth, and political activism** – parents opposed to CRT can better root out its insidious influence on their children and schools.

---

[32] "Merchant of Revolution," by Christopher Rufo, *City Journal*, April 13, 2021

[33] "'Action Civics' Replaces Citizenship with Partisanship," by Stanley Kurtz, *The American Mind*, January 26, 2021

Chapter Three: Is Critical Race Theory in Your Child's School?

"The philosophy of the school room in one generation will be the philosophy of government in the next."

-Abraham Lincoln

Understanding CRT in theory and praxis – how it's theoretical tenets developed in colleges and universities and now trickle down into K-12 schools – is only the first part in the three step process which helps parents **understand, expose, and challenge CRT**.

To successfully identify and **expose** CRT, parents must be familiar with the linguistical nuances (language games) used by activist organizations, politicians, as well as school boards and the mainstream media, which allow CRT and its various offshoots to remain in K-12 classrooms.

In order for CRT to continue to disrupt America's culture, values, and institutions (and ruin MLK's "Dream" by turning the ideals of the Civil Rights Movement on its head), it must hide under the radar where it has stayed for so long. Concerned parents must stay vigilant and continue to expose and point it out.

Game of Semantics

In June of 2021, Joy Reid invited Manhattan Institute senior fellow Christopher Rufo onto her MSNBC show, "The ReidOut," to discuss Critical Race Theory. Because Reid could not adequately debate Rufo on CRT – she constantly interrupted Rufo, refusing to let him get a word out – she chose to play a game of semantics, insisting CRT was not anywhere to be found in K-12 schools.[34]

---

[34] "Joy Reid is schooled by critical race theory critic whom she refused to let speak," Emily Jacobs, *New York Post*, June 24, 2021

She explained that "NBC has looked into this," and that Critical Race Theory was *not* being taught in K-12 schools, only in law school. Reid's claim was troubling for two reasons. One, she was woefully ignorant of the reality of CRT in America, choosing to ignore the insidious nature of CRT and allowing it to fester under the radar.

Two, it was flat out deception; she was purposely confusing theory with praxis, conflating theoretical CRT from academia with the practical application of CRT in K-12 schools. Obviously, educators in K-12 schools were not using texts authored by Kimberle Crenshaw or Richard Delgado, and teaching the theoretical tenets of CRT to students.

Reid's tactic of purposely confusing theoretical CRT in academia with its practical application in K-12 schools is the default maneuver of those who are either completely ignorant of the whole issue, or of those who advocate identity-based approaches and want CRT to remain unchallenged, where it can continue to erode traditional American culture and values. In short, those who believe America is a fundamentally racist and oppressive place, founded on White supremacy, believe that approaches like CRT are needed to fundamentally transform the nation.

Not simply *improve* it, but *transform* it. This is a point that is lost on some moderates and traditional liberals, who lean left on issues but don't realize the corrosive nature of CRT. The activists and Marxist scholars pushing CRT demand *radical change* and are calling for social, academic, and cultural *revolution*.

CRT by Any Other Name

The practical application of CRT in K-12 schools can manifest itself in multiple forms and under different names. It's important to note that instructional approaches and strategies can change from one school district to another, so the CRT-related terms that will be discussed should be evaluated on an individual school by school basis.

One way to evaluate the appropriateness of an instructional model or pedagogy is to ask the following questions: Does this approach . . .

- *stereotype or scapegoat entire groups of people?*
- *racialize instruction or the learning environment?*
- *employ racially segregated affinity groups or caucuses?*
- *target "Whiteness" or attempt to disrupt it?*

- *divide groups into "oppressors" and "oppressed"?*
- *redefine common terms or coin new ideological language?*
- *target objectivity, truth, and neutrality?*
- *indoctrinate students with a partisan agenda and encourage activism?*

If the answer is *yes* to one or more of these questions, a closer look at the curriculum or instructional model may be needed. In Chapter Five, strategies and resources for challenging CRT will be discussed.

Antiracism

The most common educational framework which uses principles of CRT is **antiracism**. Antiracism is concerned with systems over individuals. Antiracist educators, such as Robin DiAngelo and Ibram X. Kendi, believe all racial disparities in the United States are the sole result of one thing: racism.

Racist systems and policies, both conscious and unconscious, are perpetuated by privileged Whites, who benefit from this knowingly and unknowingly. Antiracists attempt to end such systems by calling out, confronting, and disrupting White privilege and so-called "White supremacy culture." In certain cases, antiracism uses discrimination to end discrimination.

As University of South Dakota sociologist Jack Niemonen wrote in his paper after doing an exhaustive analysis of 160 peer-reviewed journal articles on the subject:

> Generally, antiracist education is understood as a set of pedagogical, curricular, and organizational strategies that hope to promote racial equality by identifying, then eliminating, White privilege. . . . One of its strengths, it is claimed, is the ability to move beyond prejudice and discrimination as a problem to be corrected in individuals in order to examine critically how institutional structures support racist practices economically, politically, and culturally.[35]

---

[35] "Antiracist Education in Theory and Practice: A Critical Assessment," by Jack Niemonen, *The American Sociologist*, September 20, 2007

Antiracist programs **should:**

- Expose and end racial injustice
- Encourage multiculturalism
- Teach tolerance
- Foster understanding and communication

Antiracist programs **should not:**

- Target "Whiteness"
- Use the terms "White privilege" or "White fragility"
- Stereotype or scapegoat groups because of race
- Polarize people into "oppressors" or "oppressed"

Does the antiracism approach in your child's school incorporate troublesome elements of CRT? Ask yourself these questions:

- *Is it focused on eliminating "White privilege" or "White supremacy culture"?*
- *Does it use the term "White Fragility" or imply all Whites are systemically racist?*
- *Does it imply Whites suffer from "internalized racial superiority," or that people of color suffer from "internalized oppression"?*
- *Does it polarize groups into "oppressors" and "oppressed"?*

Equity (Or Diversity, Equity, and Inclusion)

Another approach that often contains elements of CRT is known as **equity**. Equity is not about equal opportunity – but about equal outcome. It's not concerned with a level playing field, but with level scores and level results. Under an antiracist framework, equity is zero-sum: one group must be disrupted or dismantled for another group to make gains. In some cases, K-12 schools use "equity audits" to look for patterns among identity groups (usually between Whites and students of color) in things like discipline, standardized test scores, and enrollment in classes. If disparities exist, procedures will be enacted to correct or close the gaps.

Equity, done correctly, can be a positive – as it insures equal access to resources for all children, and keeps rigor of instruction high. The devil is in the details, however. When equity *removes access* or *lowers instructional rigor*, it can become a problem. The elimination of honors or A.P. classes in schools because of disparities in enrollment among students of color – as is happening in New York City and Seattle – is one example of curtailing access.[36]

An example of equity lowering instructional rigor is Seattle's "K-12 Math Ethnic Studies Framework," which explores how Western mathematics can "disenfranchise people and communities of color" and analyzes "the ways in which ancient mathematical knowledge has been appropriated by Western culture."[37] Instead of learning math, students learn partisan social justice activism.

Another drawback of equity programs (also known as "Diversity, Equity, and Inclusion") is when correlation is used to prove causation. According to a study by the U.S. Department of Education's Office for Civil Rights, Black students are more than three times as likely as their White peers to be suspended or expelled. This is widely attributed to systemic racism, being that 84 percent of America's public school teachers are White.

But there is a lurking variable: poverty. According to statistics from the National Poverty Center, 38 percent of Black children in the United States live in poverty, whereas only 12 percent of White children are impoverished.[38] This is extremely significant because research continues to show that poverty leads to poor conduct, low academic achievement, and the chronic breaking of school rules. In other words, students from different socioeconomic backgrounds have different challenges and *do not behave the same.*

---

[36] "Gifted programs worsen inequality. Here's what happens when schools try to get rid of them," by Rachel Blustain, NBC News, October 14, 2020.

[37] "In Seattle, math is cultural appropriation," by Madeline Fry Schultz, *Washington Examiner*, October 23, 2019

[38] "Poverty Facts," University of Michigan

Yet under an *equity* approach to discipline, the root causes of poverty are ignored in favor of simply ending discipline disparities, which means the implementation of race-based discipline. In other words, racial quotas are used and skin color – not behavior – becomes the means of determining discipline measures, which in many cases disrupts the learning environment for students and hinders the educations of all children.[39]

Equity programs **should**:

- Promote programs and resources to all children
- Maintain instructional rigor
- Eliminate gaps and disparities in learning and resources

Equity programs **should not:**

- Eliminate programs or resources
- Water-down curriculum or instruction
- Use correlation to prove causation

Does the equity approach in your child's school incorporate troublesome elements of CRT? Ask yourself these questions:

- *Is "equity" eliminating programs in schools?*
- *Is "equity" lowering instructional rigor or watering-down curriculum?*
- *Is "equity" using correlation to prove causation, and using "systemic racism" as a blanket cause when there are other underlying variables that need attention?*

Culturally Responsive Teaching

Like antiracism and equity, **culturally responsive teaching** can contain troublesome elements of CRT. However, it's important to separate the positive and proactive components from the toxic elements.

---

[39] "Discipline Reform Through the Eyes of Teachers," David Griffith and Adam Tyner, Fordham Institute, July 2019

Author and educator Zaretta Hammond's book, *Culturally Responsive Teaching and The Brain: Promoting Authentic Engagement and Rigor Among Culturally and Linguistically Diverse Students*, is an example of culturally responsive teaching with genuine purpose and merit; most of the approaches in her book – like the section on building learning partnerships – are positive, and focused on communication and collaboration. Genuine culturally responsive teaching is a great way to connect with students from diverse backgrounds, and help them become successful in both the classroom and real life.

Unfortunately, not all programs dubbed "culturally responsive teaching" are genuine, and some are mere masks for programs aimed at indoctrinating students with CRT ideology or other political agendas. Take, for example, the Illinois State Board of Education's "Culturally Responsive Teaching and Leading Standards." As Stanley Kurtz, a senior fellow at the Ethics and Public Policy Center, writes:

> Teachers already pressed into the role of de facto leftist community organizers by the 2015 Illinois civics law will soon be liable to negative performance reviews; student, peer, or parent complaints; or even failure of licensure, if they refuse to lead classroom discussions or organize student protests and lobbying expeditions on behalf of leftist causes. Illinois's new Culturally Responsive Teaching and Leading Standards, in combination with the existing Illinois civics law, really do formalize the conversion of K-12 schools into political indoctrination camps. . . .
>
> The Illinois Culturally Responsive Teaching and Leading Standards are less about education than political re-education. The new rule mandates, for example, that teachers, "assess how their biases...affect...how they access tools to mitigate their own behavior (racism, sexism, homophobia, unearned privilege, Eurocentrism, etc.)" You might think it impossible to "mitigate" the "unearned privilege" of being White, male, or straight, but Bettina L. Love, a prominent advocate of Critical Race Theory in education, holds that "White Teachers Need Anti-Racist Therapy." By this she means therapy that combats "White emotionalities" or what Robin DiAngelo famously calls "White fragility." The committee that drafted the new rule includes an article touting white fragility training sessions to help teachers "move past their Whiteness" in the readings it offers to explain the standards.[40]

---

[40] "Ultra-Woke Illinois Mandates Are Top Threat to U.S. Education," by Stanley Kurtz, *National Review*, January 19, 2021

As Stanley Kurtz reveals, the Illinois Culturally Responsive Teaching and Leading Standards are infested with nearly ever principle of CRT mentioned previously (Chapter Two), from color-consciousness, to the opposition to Whiteness, to the use of Marxism, to the unabashed promotion of political activism.

Culturally responsive teaching **should**:

- Foster communication
- Deepen student-teacher relationships
- Build learning partnerships
- Help students of all cultures engage in learning

Culturally responsive teaching **should not:**

- Target Whiteness
- Indoctrinate students on issues
- Promote political activism
- Organize protests or lobby for partisan causes

Does the culturally responsive teaching in your child's school incorporate troublesome elements of CRT? Ask yourself these questions:

- *Does the culturally responsive teaching in your child's school target "Whiteness"?*
- *Does the culturally responsive teaching in your child's school indoctrinate students on issues?*
- *Does the culturally responsive teaching in your child's school push a political agenda or promote political activism?*
- *Does the culturally responsive teaching in your child's school require students to organize protests or lobby for partisan causes?*

The 1619 Project and 'Accurate History'

Those pushing Critical Race Theory in K-12 schools insist students must learn "accurate history," especially when it comes to racism and slavery. Nikole Hannah-Jones's 1619 Project, published by *The New York Times*, is at the center of this debate. The irony is that the 1619 Project, as acknowledged by Hannah-Jones herself, is not history so much as it is social justice activism.

In other words, objectivity has been replaced with a kind of subjective truth that aims to bring awareness to past injustice, whether or not this injustice is factual, metaphorical, or arrived upon through revisionism. Which means the events portrayed in the 1619 Project are not "accurate" from a traditional historical perspective, but from a "subjective" one, which is a hallmark of Critical Race Theory.

John McWhorter, an African American professor of linguistics at Columbia University, takes issue with the historical facts at the center of the "1619 Project." As McWhorter writes in *Reason Magazine*:

> The verdict is in: The idea that America's real founding was in 1619 does not wash. And yet, it will be considered a mark of sophistication to pretend otherwise.
>
> Since last August, *The New York Times* has asked us to consider that America's real founding was not in 1776 but in 1619, when the first Africans were brought to these shores. Nikole Hannah-Jones teaches that the Revolutionary War was fought mainly not to escape British tyranny, but out of fear that British tyranny was about to threaten the institution of slavery.[41]

In a *Wall Street Journal* article titled "The '1619 Project' Gets Schooled," Elliot Kaufman further elaborates on the criticisms of well-respected scholars and historians:

> "So wrong in so many ways" is how Gordon Wood, the Pulitzer Prize-winning historian of the American Revolution, characterized the New York Times's "1619 Project." James McPherson, dean of Civil War historians and another Pulitzer winner, said the Times presented an "unbalanced, one-sided account" that "left most of the history out." Even more surprising than the criticism from these generally liberal historians was where the interviews appeared: on the World Socialist Web Site, run by the Trotskyist Socialist Equality Party.[42]

---

[41] "The 1619 Project Depicts an America Tainted by Original Sin," by John McWhorter, *Reason Magazine*, January 30, 2020

[42] "The '1619 Project' Gets Schooled," by Gordon Wood, *Wall Street Journal*, December 16, 2019

In an Atlantic article titled "A Matter of Facts," Sean Wilentz, Professor of history at Princeton University, detailed the letter he wrote to *The New York Times*, requesting the publication correct its basic mistakes:

> On December 20, the *Times Magazine* published a letter that I signed with four other historians — Victoria Bynum, James McPherson, James Oakes, and Gordon Wood. Our letter applauded the project's stated aim to raise public awareness and understanding of slavery's central importance in our history. Although the project is not a conventional work of history and cannot be judged as such, the letter intended to help ensure that its efforts did not come at the expense of basic accuracy. Offering practical support to that end, it pointed out specific statements that, if allowed to stand, would misinform the public and give ammunition to those who might be opposed to the mission of grappling with the legacy of slavery. The letter requested that the *Times* print corrections of the errors that had already appeared, and that it keep those errors from appearing in any future materials published with the Times' imprimatur, including the school curricula the newspaper announced it was developing in conjunction with the project.[43]

Curiously, *The New York Times* chose to let the flawed revisionist history stand in an effort at bringing awareness to past racial injustice. But as America's leading historians have pointed out, altering facts to forward so-called social justice causes is in fact doing a disservice to the cause itself.

Teaching America's youth inaccurate depictions of America's past isn't going to help educate them as knowledgeable and informed citizens. Accuracy of information is necessary to allow students to think critically about the world around them, and altering such information – in the name of social justice – is not providing children the resources they need to become proactive, self-empowered learners.

History textbooks which highlight America's past sins are plentiful. There is no need to fabricate or create such history.

Teaching accurate history **should**:

- Be *objectively* accurate, based in historical records

---

[43] A Matter of Facts," by Sean Wilentz, *The Atlantic*, January 22, 2020

- Be fair and balanced, revealing both positive and negative accounts
- Incorporate the histories of diverse cultures

Teaching accurate history **should not**:

- Alter factually accurate historical records
- Revise history through a "subjective" lens
- Disproportionally represent historical accounts

Does the history being taught in your child's school incorporate troublesome elements of CRT? Ask yourself these questions:

- *Does the teaching of "accurate history" in your child's school involve using the historically inaccurate 1619 Project?*
- *Does the teaching of "accurate history" in your child's school involve altering factually accurate historical records by changing events to fit a political narrative?*
- *Does the teaching of "accurate history" in your child's school disproportionally represent negative historical accounts of America's founding, or reinterpret America's founding principles or ideals?*

Black Lives Matter at School

In the fight for racial justice, the slogan "Black lives matter" is an admirable mantra that most Americans embrace; creating a fair and inclusive society is indeed a very worthy goal.

But Black Lives Matter the activist organization with a registered political action committee is a different matter entirely.[44] And it's Black Lives Matter the political organization that is pushing an agenda-driven curriculum into America's K-12 schools, an agenda based in CRT and neo-Marxism that at times is not only racially polarizing, but calls for defunding police; disrupting the nuclear family; and replacing individualism and capitalism with an irresponsible brand of socialism.

---

[44] "Black Lives Matter launches a political action committee," by Maya King, *Politico*, October 9, 2020

At the center of the BLM "School Starter Kit" are the group's "13 Guiding Principles," one of which is "globalism," and another "Black Villages," the former concerned with replacing nationalism with a blend of world-wide socialism, and the latter with deconstructing the "Western nuclear family."[45] This is quite puzzling, being that 50 years of educational and sociological research shows that children who come from a two-parent nuclear family do better on every academic and behavior measure than those kids who come from a non-nuclear family.[46]

A deeper dive into the curriculum itself is eye-opening. BLM's elementary school lesson plan includes a resource titled "Activism, Organizing and Resistance," which instructs third-grade art teachers to help their students become community activists, literally. In a lesson titled "Art and Community Activism," along with an activity called "Who Are the Activists in My Community?", children are taught to make activist signs and murals, all supporting the pre-established BLM globalist, anti-police, anti-nuclear family agenda.[47]

The lessons for third-graders go on to teach "resistance stories," explore the usefulness of "teacher strikes," and require children to deconstruct their racial and gender identities through identity maps and puzzles.[48]

The middle school BLM curriculum has pre-adolescents answer the essential question: "How has historical oppression lead to racial injustice in today's criminal justice system?" From here these children are asked to imagine "a world with no police" by completing a free-writing exercise, and offers teachers a resource document called "Teaching About Controversial or Difficult Issues" which promotes the college level book *The New Jim Crow*.[49]

"Students and teachers can read this chapter to explore how many police departments 'seek and destroy' in some neighborhoods while they 'protect and serve' in others," the resources states.

---

[45] https://docs.google.com/document/d/1kjnmt8y-7d0_8y6eVxRG_OeGv5Sy4yHudDIpmiaoLFg/edit

[46] "The Family – America's Smallest School," Paul E. Barton & Richard J. Coley, ETS, 2007

[47] https://docs.google.com/document/d/1zk2lywRHXX32s90PF_jggLttX5YhWOVh2q5vR9Rak7A/edit

[48] https://docs.google.com/document/d/1zk2lywRHXX32s90PF_jggLttX5YhWOVh2q5vR9Rak7A/edit

[49] https://drive.google.com/drive/folders/1LGslwJwhXvpVnDgw0uC-n794l6EGzpuH

The BLM high school curriculum offers ways to embed the activist group's agenda in all subjects – including math – and in English class, offers an article titled "White People Hate Protests," complete with pictures of police man-handling Blacks from the 1960s. This article is supplemented by a resource on LBJ's Riot Commission, an activity that insinuates that property destruction is okay if it's done for the right reasons. The lesson is complete with discussion questions, one of which asks: *Name 2-3 causes of the riots you feel were most important. Explain your selections.*[50]

Also included in the high school curriculum is Danez Smith's "Dear White America."[51] The lines "we did not ask to be part of your America" and "your master magic trick, America. Now he's breathing, now he don't. Abra-cadaver. White bread voodoo," is particularly concerning.

This is only a small slice of BLM's curriculum, which is neo-Marxist Critical Race Theory at its root. It's designed to teach students *what* to think, not *how* to think, ignores most literacy and skills-based instruction, and aims to turn children into future activists who will carry the political agenda into the next generation.

Is BLM's neo-Marxist curriculum, based in CRT, being used in your child's school? Ask yourself these questions:

- *Does curriculum in your child's school advocate defunding police or law enforcement?*
- *Does curriculum in your child's school advocate disrupting the nuclear family, or erasing language used to describe "traditional families"?*
- *Does curriculum in your child's school advocate socialism/globalism, or disparage capitalism, individualism, or meritocracy?*

Red Flags For Concerned Parents

Parents should approach with caution curriculum that includes one or more of the following:

---

[50] https://drive.google.com/drive/folders/1R4s6TVN1zt3uVHrCLeGR6BKr2AXPlMnx

[51] https://www.youtube.com/watch?v=LSp4v294xog

Any material related to Ibram X. Kendi (*How to Be an Antiracist*) or Robin DiAngelo (*White Fragility*). These books are extremely polarizing, agenda-driven, and divide people into identity groups – judging them by the color of their skin, and not the content of their character, and have no place in K-12 schools. These books may even violate federal anti-discrimination laws, and should be met with extreme caution.

Any activity, lesson, or material that uses the phrase "White privilege," "White fragility," or so-called "White supremacy." These materials polarize and judge students by race, and may also violate federal anti-discrimination laws.

Any activity, lesson, or material that uses the phrase "anti-Blackness," or encourages a student to admit to or acknowledge their anti-Blackness. Such language is confusing and extremely polarizing, and has no place in a K-12 school.

Any curriculum that focuses too heavily on identity, or has children dissect or analyze their identity, or complete an identity map or identity wheel. These activities incorporate the problematic use of "deconstruction," violate student privacy, and polarize by race.

Any curriculum that targets "Whiteness," or asks students to disrupt or deconstruct "Whiteness," "White privilege," or so-called "White supremacy." Such material is traumatizing, racially polarizing, and in violation of federal anti-discrimination laws.

Any lesson or activity that divides or polarizes students by race – splitting students into so-called "affinity groups" or "caucuses." This is neo-segregation, and promotes racial polarization.

Any lesson or activity that uses or includes the 1619 Project, which is historically inaccurate. Accuracy of information is necessary to allow students to think critically about the world around them, and altering such information – in the name of social justice – is not providing children the resources they need to become proactive, self-empowered learners.

Any lesson or activity that uses or includes Black Lives Matter curriculum, which is agenda-driven, polarizing, and based in partisan politics. BLM advocates defunding police and law enforcement, disrupting the nuclear family, and attacks capitalism, individualism, and meritocracy.

CRT: District vs. Classroom Level

Just as Critical Race Theory can camouflage itself under different names – and CRT advocates can use semantics to keep it under the radar – a school district can appear to be free of CRT, but these toxic and polarizing concepts can still show up in your child's school. As such, it is imperative that parents stay abreast of policies and curriculum at the state and district level, as well as keep an eye on activities and lessons that are directly taking place in the classroom.

The pushback against CRT at the state level has been impressive. As of July 2021, 28 states have attempted to enact policies to rein in the teaching of CRT.[52] Likewise, scores of concerned parents across the nation – of all races and political backgrounds – have gotten active in the fight against CRT, organizing parent groups, speaking out at school board meetings, and educating themselves on school policy in an effort to save their schools.

But again, the absence of CRT at the state or local level doesn't mean your child's school is in the clear. Most school districts give teachers flexibility when it comes to designing lessons, as long as the lessons support state-mandated standards and learning objectives. And although most school districts require teachers to get approval before using textbooks and other teaching materials, supplementary materials and so-called "teacher resources" (which are often supplied by activist groups like BLM) can come in through the backdoor.

And it's through these "teacher resources," supplied by groups like BLM, that educators can go rogue and still implement CRT and other critical pedagogy in their lessons. In May of 2021, Alaska Governor Mike Dunleavy tweeted the following about CRT:

> One of the greatest dangers posed to our nation is focusing on a message of division. Critical Race Theory is a false narrative that ignores our history of striving to improve. It has no place in our schools.

---

[52] "Efforts to restrict teaching about racism and bias have multiplied across the U.S.," by Cathryn Stout & Gabrielle LaMarr LeMee, *Chalkbeat*, July 22, 2021

The following month, 14 Alaska teachers signed a nationwide pledge from the Zinn Education Project to teach through the lens of Critical Race Theory regardless of any legislation barring it.[53]

In short, parents must pay close attention to the daily activities taking place in their child's classroom, as well as the curriculum approved by the state and local school board.

---

[53] "Efforts to restrict teaching about racism and bias have multiplied across the U.S.," by Cathryn Stout & Gabrielle LaMarr LeMee, *Chalkbeat*, July 22, 2021

Chapter Four: Identity-Based vs. Principle-Based Approaches

*"We must adjust to changing times
and still hold to unchanging principles."*

-Jimmy Carter

Two of the biggest drawbacks of Critical Race Theory are that it regards **truth as subjective**, and that it strictly adheres to **cultural relativism**. Both concepts are flawed and ultimately result in **cultural separatism**.

First, CRT's flawed concept of truth. As was stated previously, truth itself is not subjective – *perception* of truth is. You could fill a glass halfway, and from one perspective it's half full, and from another perspective it's half empty. But the *truth* is that it's half empty *and* half full. Both perspectives are part of the whole glass, and it's the whole glass that joins them together. The truth, then, is the whole glass.

Another analogy is the perception of a beach ball. If there were a giant beach ball sitting between a group of people, and each person were asked what color it was from their perspective, you might get five or six different answers. Some may argue emphatically that it's yellow, while others may insist it's blue, and on a relative level, these are both true. But this does not make truth relative.

The absolute truth, underlying all of these perspectives, is that the beach ball is yellow, and blue, and green, and white, and orange, and red. All perspectives are part of the whole ball, and it's the whole ball that joins them together. The truth, then, is the whole ball.

Unfortunately, the cynical nature of CRT conflates absolute truth with relative perception, and insists instead that *truth itself is relative*, which denies the underlying absolute nature of truth.

This leads to CRT's second major drawback – the strict adherence to cultural relativism. Cultural relativism is the idea that to truly understand another culture, one must view it on its own terms and not make judgments using the standards of another culture (all cultures are equally valid and unique). And while this can indeed foster understanding and tolerance for diversity, Critical Race Theory has used cultural relativism to argue that shared universal values are impossible, because any "shared universal value" is really just another form of White supremacy culture.

In other words, Whites are the dominant group in society, so no matter what values are arrived upon, these values will be biased in favor of Whites and against people of color, even if all cultures came together and attempted to create mutually agreed upon values. *All values, therefore, are culturally relative.*

The result of this strict resistance to anything shared or universal is **cultural separatism**, which is a kind of "us vs. them" based on a person's identity (race, religion, gender, sexuality, etc.). Because CRT insists we are hopelessly restricted by our own cultures and relative perspectives, and can never truly bond on a universal or human level, we must as a result be forever race-conscious and continue to view the world and everything in it through the lens of race and identity.

An Identity-Based Approach

Critical Theory – and by extension, Critical Race Theory – has made America obsessed with identity (*Cynical Theories*, by Helen Pluckrose and James Lindsey, is an excellent book on this topic). In 2021, we are not only overly race-conscious, but are now hyper-focused on religion, gender, and sexuality, among other emerging identity groups.

In July of 2021, the National Education Association adopted what they termed "Business Item 39," which pledged to "provide an already-created, in-depth, study that critiques empire, White supremacy, anti-Blackness, anti-Indigeneity, racism, patriarchy, cisheteropatriarchy, capitalism, ableism, anthropocentrism, and other forms of power and oppression at the intersections of our society . . ."[54]

---

[54] "Largest Teachers' Union Erases Campaign to Push Critical Race Theory from Website," by Caroline Downey, *National Review*, July 6, 2021

Instead of finding common bonds between all Americans, the NEA, like so many other organizations indoctrinated in CRT, are going in the complete *opposite* direction: they are using deconstruction to break society down into smaller and smaller identity groups, so they can effectively reconstruct them into so-called "allies" that will push an approved political agenda and forward the greater ideological vision of CRT.

Identity-based approaches perpetuate the myth that a failure to center race in society (or to see everything through the lens of race and identity), will result in a failure to see racism and racial injustice. Put another way, it forwards the false notion that society thinks race *doesn't* matter, when in reality, society thinks race *shouldn't* matter. An emphasis on race-consciousness is *not* needed to see racial injustice, or to see harmful patterns or racial disparities. Principles and values can accomplish this, as will be described in the next section.

Identity-based approaches have the following characteristics:

- Focus on systems and collectivism
- Make broad generalizations and stereotype entire groups of people
- Are polarizing and based in dichotomy
- Operate on a political level and are concerned with policy
- Believe change comes through activism and political organizing
- Believe quality of life stems from government
- Believe identity is the primary determinant of success

Identity-based approaches focus on systems and push collectivism. Identity-based approaches (like those of Ibram X. Kendi and Robin DiAngelo), teach problems are institutional, and solutions lie in fixing "systems." Often times correlation is used to prove causation, which may lead to inaccurate fixes and policy proposals.

For example, systemic racism is usually viewed as the sole cause of racial disparities, despite many complex underlying variables (like poverty and behavior when it comes to the disparities in school discipline). The ultimate goal is a more collectivist society (socialism/communism), where government, political lobbyists, and large private agencies backed by politicians can centralize control and gain more reach and power.

Identity-based approaches make broad generalizations and stereotype entire groups of people. Common generalizations under CRT (an identity-based model) are that Whites are inherently racist, privileged, and anti-Black, and that people of color are victims who suffer from internalized oppression.[55] Incredibly, Critical Race Theory has completely deconstructed the concepts of "stereotyping" and "generalizing," turning them from negatives to be avoided into positives that must be accepted. Robin DiAngelo even goes as far as saying that as a trained sociologist, it's okay for her to generalize about White people.

Identity-based approaches are polarizing and based in dichotomy. The use of Marxism to polarize entire groups of people into "oppressors" and "oppressed" is a hallmark of identity-based models. Likewise, the constant insistence that universal values are not possible – and that all things are relative to culture and identity – leads to cultural separatism, and further polarizes society.

Identity-based approaches operate on a political level and are concerned with policy. Ibram X. Kendi, bestselling author of *How To Be An Antiracist*, is head of Boston University's Center for Antiracist Research, which recently received a $10 million donation from Twitter CEO Jack Dorsey.

According to Kendi, the mission of the center is to "foster exhaustive racial research, research-based policy innovation, data-driven educational and advocacy campaigns, and narrative-change initiatives."[56] In other words, he aims to change policy and influence narrative through politics. In 2019, Kendi wrote an article in *Politico Magazine* titled, "Pass an Antiracist Constitutional Amendment, which stated:

---

[55] *What Does It Mean To Be White?: Developing White Racial Literacy*, by Robin DiAngelo

[56] BU Center For Antiracist Research, https://www.bu.edu/antiracism-center/

To fix the original sin of racism, Americans should pass an anti-racist amendment to the U.S. Constitution that enshrines two guiding anti-racist principals: Racial inequity is evidence of racist policy and the different racial groups are equals. The amendment would make unconstitutional racial inequity over a certain threshold, as well as racist ideas by public officials (with "racist ideas" and "public official" clearly defined). It would establish and permanently fund the Department of Anti-racism (DOA) comprised of formally trained experts on racism and no political appointees. The DOA would be responsible for preclearing all local, state and federal public policies to ensure they won't yield racial inequity, monitor those policies, investigate private racist policies when racial inequity surfaces, and monitor public officials for expressions of racist ideas. The DOA would be empowered with disciplinary tools to wield over and against policymakers and public officials who do not voluntarily change their racist policy and ideas.[57]

Identity-based approaches believe change comes through activism and political organizing. When the focus is on systems and not individuals, change is achieved through activism and organizing, not on interpersonal skill building. "Action civics," as previously discussed, is an example of this identity-based approach. Unfortunately, since the emergence of CRT, being a good citizen is not about an objective understanding of America's founding principles and Constitutional system, but about lobbying and getting active for partisan causes.

Identity-based approaches believe quality of life stems from government. Unfortunately, identity-based approaches believe that systems, policy, and skin color are the keys to success, and that average people aren't able to be the captain of their own ship. The key to having a good quality of life stems from policy, systemic justice, and by default *government*, which has the ultimate power to make policies and control the system.

Identity-based approaches believe identity is the primary determinant of success. Skin color – as well as religion, gender, sexuality, and how these manifest through "intersectionality" – are the things that determine a person's success in life, not individual values, principles, choices, or life priorities.

---

[57] "Pass an Antiracist Constitutional Amendment," by Ibram X. Kendi, *Politico Magazine*, 2019

Tragically, America's cultural gatekeepers have adopted an identity-based approach, which is why the mainstream media, academia, the entertainment industry, Big Tech, and corporate America have been pushing and promoting Critical Race Theory so heavily. They do so to remain fashionable (to virtue signal), to avoid peer pressure (to escape getting "cancelled"), and for opportunity (to take advantage of the impressive power and money available within the networks that push CRT, like Black Lives Matter).

A Principle-Based Approach

A principle-based approach is the polar opposite of an identity-based approach, as it moves past the superficial notions of race, religion, gender, and sexuality, to a deeper, more universal place of communion and understanding. In short, it continues the legacy of the Civil Rights Movement, and espouses MLK's traditional ideal of color-blindness (before it was deconstructed and then falsely reconstructed by critical race theorists).

A principle-based approach does NOT have the two major drawbacks of CRT, **as it views truth as objective and absolute, and believes that there are human values that are indeed universal** – that transcend race, religion, gender, and sexuality.

These universal values include things like: tolerance, empathy, compassion, patience, trust, kindness, love, integrity, dignity, etc. These values are at the core of a person's principles, and help build the skills needed to have a manageable, good quality of life. Such values and principles help develop: communication, active listening, organization, service, anger management, time management, self-reflection, family and community involvement, and being proactive, among many other positives.

Although principle-based approaches do not focus on identity, they still allow educators to see overall demographic patterns, to address racial disparities and injustice, and work toward diversity. Thus, **the myth that a failure to center race in society (or to see everything through the lens of race and identity), will result in a failure to see racism and racial injustice, is effectively dismissed.**

Principle-based approaches have the following characteristics:

- Focus on people and individuals
- Are unifying and based in synergy
- Are based in the American experiment of individual freedom and liberty
- Believe change comes through personal skill building and self-improvement
- Believe quality of life stems from personal choices and priorities
- Believe principles and values are the primary determinant of success

Principle-based approaches focus on people and individuals. Principle-based approaches do not overgeneralize or stereotype entire groups of people. They strive to interact with people on a personal level, and treat everyone as a *unique individual*, not as a member of an identity group. As such, Whites are not regarded as inherently racist or privileged, and are not blamed or scapegoated for past historical transgressions. Likewise, people of color are not regarded as suffering from internalized oppression, and are not seen as a monolith of victimhood. Individual strengths and weaknesses are recognized and addressed, which encourages proactive independence and self-reliance, and not racial resentment.

Principle-based approaches are unifying and based in synergy. Because principle-based approaches don't categorize people by race and identity (or as "oppressors" and "oppressed"), they do not create an atmosphere of polarization. Instead, they use underlying values and principles to bring individuals together, and focus on the ways *people are the same*. Once this bonding happens, a larger synergy is created, as the whole suddenly becomes larger than the parts.

Principle-based approaches are rooted in the American experiment of individual freedom and liberty. America was founded on the ideals of individual freedom, liberty, and the right to pursue happiness. Although historically, these ideals were not properly given to everyone, this does not mean the ideals themselves are not worth pursuing.

While an identity-based approach such as CRT attacks America's fundamental ideals as hypocritical – insisting they must be radically transformed through collective resistance and even revolution – a principle-based approach believes that these ideals are worth preserving. Through fundamental values, *all* groups can have an equal shot at the American Dream.

Principle-based approaches believe change comes through personal skill building and self-improvement. Principle-based approaches believe *all change is self-change*. While there is a place for political action and lobbying for policy, the primary concern should be on personal skill building and self-improvement. Personal, family, and community responsibility should always come first.

Principle-based approaches believe quality of life stems from personal choices and priorities. Personal choices have consequences, and play a bigger and more immediate part in a person's life than most any system. Manageability and quality of life are directly rooted in choices and priorities, and principle-based approaches center on these direct pathways to personal freedom and happiness. Personal choices and priorities can also help change society for the better, too.

Principle-based approaches believe principles and values are the primary determinant of success. Principle-based approaches create a moral foundation for life, and do not change depending on a person's racial identity, or the ever-changing equation of so-called "intersectionality." Universal principles and values are real – transcend race, religion, gender, and sexuality – and can always be accessed at any time, and for any reason. They are the key to liberation from the bonds of collective identity, from fashionable groupthink, and most importantly, from the toxic tenets of Critical Race Theory.

Principle-Based Educators and Programs

Because principle-based approaches are not partisan and do not revolve around community organizing and political activism, they tend to go unnoticed and remain under the radar. Unlike identity-based models – which aim to agitate, anger, and provoke people into taking "action" – principle-based approaches are considered boring and unfashionable, do not feed egos, and provide minimal opportunity to tap into the incredibly large and powerful network of CRT. Rejecting an identity-based approach for a principle-based one might even get you cancelled.

Still, educators and programs that forego a hyper-focus on race-consciousness and instead center on deeper skills and values do exist. Below are some that can serve as alternatives to the polarizing identity-based models saturating K-12 schools across America.

The values-based **1776 Unites**, founded by Bob Woodson, "is a movement to liberate tens of millions of Americans by helping them become agents of their own uplift and transformation, by embracing the true founding values of our country."

As stated on their website:

> The 1776 Unites curriculum offers authentic, inspiring stories from American history that show what is best in our national character and what our freedom makes possible even in the most difficult circumstances. 1776 Unites maintains a special focus on stories that celebrate Black excellence, reject victimhood culture, and showcase African-Americans who have prospered by embracing America's founding ideals.[58]

The **Woodson Center**, also founded by Bob Woodson, is dedicated to "Transforming lives, schools, and troubled neighborhoods from the inside out by involving those suffering the problem, empowering local leaders to identify capacities of residents and help them to achieve their potential."[59]

Some programs at The Woodson Center are "Violence Free Zones," "Training and Technical Assistance," and "Woodson Center Fellows Program," among others.

The work of **Thomas Sowell**, economist, historian, philosopher, and one of the greatest social theorists America has ever produced, is an invaluable resource for those interested in principle-based approaches and solutions. Over the past 60 years, he's published more than 40 books and written thousands of articles covering economic history, political philosophy, social inequality, education, and race.

As Jason Riley, senior fellow at the Manhattan Institute, writes:

> His name is Thomas Sowell, and he might be the most important scholar you've never heard of. . . .

---

[58] 1776 Unites, https://1776unites.com

[59] The Woodson Center, https://woodsoncenter.org

In books like *Race and Culture*, Sowell has demonstrated racial preferences are counterproductive; that political power is not necessary to advance economically; and that racial discrimination cannot be used as a blanket explanation for disparities in employment, education, and income.

He's also shown how a racial or ethnic group's self-development – acquiring certain attitudes and behaviors – has far more bearing on economic advancement than how a group is treated by society at large. The Chinese in Malaysia and the Jews in Eastern Europe are among many examples of minority groups who have risen economically, despite being the targets of bias and discrimination.

To those who use racism as an all-purpose explanation for racial inequality, Sowell's views have made him a pariah. Unable to counter his rigorous, evidence-based scholarship, left-leaning intellectuals, political activists, and mainstream media prefer to ignore him. That's why so many people today are aware of names like Ta-Nehisi Coates, Ibram X. Kendi, and Cornel West – but not Thomas Sowell.[60]

In July 2020, **Baylor University sociology professor George Yancey** wrote a very powerful critique of white fragility and antiracism titled, "Not White Fragility, Mutual Responsibility," where he proposed having a true dialogue on race relations, not merely a monologue disguised as a conversation. Named the **Mutual Accountability Approach**, Yancey suggested using sociological research (Intergroup Contact Theory based in active listening) to unify rather than divide, making solutions win-win rather than win-lose.

He states, "We have to work with each other to find win-win solutions instead of relying on win-lose scenarios. I need to hear from Whites about their concerns and they have to listen to me about mine. Only then can we work towards fashioning solutions to the racialized problems in our society that can serve all of us well."

At the center of Yancey's mutual accountability approach is active listening. Yancey writes:

---

[60] "The Great Thomas Sowell," by Jason Riley, *PragerU*, July 26, 2021

If you rely merely on accusation, blaming and canceling to compel Whites to support you, we will get what we have gotten thus far. Some Whites will respond to that. Others will engage in a backlash. Others will simply ignore us. I run into plenty of Whites who are not insensitive to the plight of people of color, but have been called racist one time too many and now want nothing to do with anything antiracist or with ideas such as white fragility.[61]

Dr. Yancey has two books that can serve as alternatives to CRT and other identity-based models:

One is called, ***Beyond Racial Gridlock: Embracing Mutual Responsibility***. Here is a brief description:

Surveys a range of approaches to racial healing that Christians have used and offers a new model for moving forward. The first part of the book analyzes four secular models regarding race used by Christians (colorblindness, Anglo-conformity, multiculturalism and White responsibility) and shows how each has its own advantages and limitations. Part two offers a new "mutual responsibility" model, which acknowledges that both majority and minority cultures have their own challenges, tendencies, and sins to repent of, and that people of different races approach racial reconciliation and justice in differing but complementary ways.

The other is called ***Transcending Racial Barriers: Toward a Mutual Obligations Approach***. Here is a brief description:

Offers a fresh perspective on how to combat racial division. Dr. Michael Emerson and Dr. Yancey look at modern efforts to overcome the racialized nature of our society. They offers what is at once a balanced approach towards dealing with racial alienation and a bold step forward in the debate about the steps necessary to overcome present-day racism.

A group called **Moral Courage ED**, founded by professor of leadership, Irshad Manji, is a solid resource for those interested in a more principle-based approach. The group's mantra is "Diversity Without Division," and states:

[61] "Not White Fragility, Mutual Responsibility," by George Yancey, Patheos.com, July 16, 2020

Society is increasingly diverse and polarized at the same time. Now more than ever, secondary school students need tools to resist the lure of an Us-Against-Them mindset.

And because most educators have never been taught to engage highly emotional issues, they, too, need tools to create brave spaces where students can disagree productively.

For schools and districts that seek to unify their communities though authentic inclusion, Moral Courage ED has offerings that are research-backed and road-tested.[62]

The Carson Scholarship Fund, founded by Dr. Ben Carson, is an excellent resource to help young people of all races tap into their potential through a love of reading and a commitment to academic excellence.

Dr. Ben's book, *Think Big: Unleashing Your Potential For Excellence*, is another great resource to help young people succeed using a principle-based approach.

The 7 Habits of Highly Effective Teens by Sean Covey, is a classic resource for teaching young people how to be proactive instead of reactive; to seek first to understand and then be understood; to think win-win; and to synergize, among other habits. After nearly 25 years, these habits have proven to be universal, and do not depend on race or identity to be effective.

These are just some of the resources and programs available that believe values are more important than identity when it comes to achieving success and maintaining a manageable, good quality of life.

---

[62] Moral Courage ED, https://moralcourage-ed.org

Chapter Five: Resources for Concerned Parents

"Let us ask ourselves, 'What kind of people do we think we are?' And let us answer, 'Free people, worthy of freedom and determined not only to remain so but to help others gain their freedom as well.'"

-Ronald Reagan

To win the most important educational battle of our lifetime – the fight against Critical Race Theory – concerned parents need the knowledge, tools, and resources to **understand, expose, and challenge CRT in their schools**.

Organizations Fighting CRT

American Enterprise Institute (AEI) is a public policy think tank dedicated "to defending human dignity, expanding human potential, and building a freer and safer world." The work of their scholars and staff "advances ideas rooted in our belief in democracy, free enterprise, American strength and global leadership, solidarity with those at the periphery of our society, and a pluralistic, entrepreneurial culture."

AEI's website (https://www.aei.org) offers helpful policy reports, research, news articles, and a schedule of AEI events. Their educational reports often target CRT and highlight ways to challenge it.

Chinese American Citizen's Alliance of Greater New York aims to "empower Chinese Americans, as citizens of the United States of America, by advocacy for Chinese-American interests based on the principles of fairness and equal opportunity, and guided by the ideals of patriotism, civility, dedication to family and culture, and the highest ethical and moral standards."

CACAGNY's website (http://www.cacagny.org/home.html) offers a schedule of events, and ways to get involved with the group's activities.

Foundation For Individual Rights In Education (FIRE) aims to "defend and sustain the individual rights of students and faculty members at America's colleges and universities. These rights include freedom of speech, freedom of association, due process, legal equality, religious liberty, and sanctity of conscience – the essential qualities of liberty."

FIRE's website (https://www.thefire.org) provides legal assistance for educators, offers news on free speech issues, which include: guides on student rights on campus; faculty rights and resources; and ways to submit a case, among other information.

Heterodox Academy is a group of over 5,000 professors, administrators, K-12 educators, staff and students who believe "diverse viewpoints and open inquiry are critical to research and learning." They aspire to create college classrooms and campuses that "welcome diverse people with diverse viewpoints and that equip learners with the habits of heart and mind to engage that diversity in open inquiry and constructive disagreement."

HA's website (https://heterodoxacademy.org) offers podcasts, blogs, teacher resources and curriculum to help foster objective critical thinking in classrooms.

Moms for Liberty is a group that "welcomes all moms, dads, grandparents and community members that have a desire to stand up for parental rights at all levels of government." They are using their first-hand knowledge and experience "to unite parents who are ready to fight those that stand in the way of liberty."

MFL's website (https://www.momsforliberty.org) offers information on chapters, meetings, and how to stop indoctrination of students in K-12 schools – especially as it relates to CRT.

No Left Turn in Education is a grassroots movement of "common-sense parents, families and citizens." Their mission is "to revive in American K-12 education the fundamental discipline of critical and active thinking based on facts, investigation, logic and sound reasoning."

NLTE's website (https://www.noleftturn.us) offers alternative curriculum, resources on state legislation tracking, sample school board letters and petitions, sample FOI (freedom of information) requests, and other valuable documents and information.

Pacific Legal Foundation is a nonprofit legal organization "that defends Americans' liberties when threatened by government overreach and abuse." Every year, PLF "represents hundreds of Americans, free of charge, who seek to improve their lives but are stymied by government. We give them their day in court to vindicate their rights and set a lasting precedent to protect everyone else."

PLF's website (https://pacificlegal.org) specializes in property rights, free speech, economic liberty, equality before the law, and the separation of powers. It also takes an interest in CRT discrimination in public schools, and recently organized a lawsuit against Thomas Jefferson High School in Fairfax, Virginia.

Parents Defending Education is a national grassroots organization "working to reclaim our schools from activists imposing harmful agendas." Through network and coalition building, investigative reporting, litigation, and engagement on local, state, and national policies, they "are fighting indoctrination in the classroom – and promoting the restoration of a healthy, non-political education for our kids."

PDE's website (https://defendinged.org) offers a three step approach: empower, expose, and engage. PDE offers information on parent and student rights, public school law (Title IX and Title XI), how to speak up at school board meetings, opt out of classes, and how to document your child's issue in school. They also have a public records letter generator, a guide to state freedom of information laws, and a FOIA procedures and guidelines manual.

Finally, they have an impressive trove of resources to help parents engage with school boards, politicians, and the public, which include: How to Create a Press Release; How to Speak to Your School Board; Questions to Ask School Officials; How to Engage with the Media; How to Run for School Board; The Importance of Winning Your PTA; and How to File a Complaint with the Office for Civil Rights at the U.S. Department of Education, among others.

Purple for Parents is a group that "informs, advocates, and engages Hoosiers to protect children from harmful agendas saturating the education system." PFP believes "the responsibility of teaching morals and values to children are the parents/caregivers and NOT a government institution." They also state America's children "are increasingly influenced by programs designed to separate their beliefs from what is taught in their home and toward a progressive understanding for the sake of social justice."

PFP's website (https://purpleforparentsindiana.com) offers analysis and education on important educational issues, and provides documents and resources for opting out of curriculum, and challenging what it calls a harmful "social justice agenda" based in CRT.

Schoolhouse Rights is a legal group whose mission is to "defend and support the individual rights of students, parents, and faculty members in public K-12 education. Freedom of speech and association, due process, legal equality, religious liberty, sanctity of conscience, and the right of parents to guide and direct the upbringing of their children are rights essential to liberty and a free society. Schoolhouse Rights defends these rights through litigation and advocacy on behalf of students, parents, and teachers in public education."

SR's website (https://schoolhouserights.org) offers an excellent "CRT checklist" for parents to see if their child's rights are being violated.

The Heritage Foundation is an organization whose mission is "to formulate and promote conservative public policies based on the principles of free enterprise, limited government, individual freedom, traditional American values, and a strong national defense."

HF's website (https://www.heritage.org) offers an excellent policy report on CRT, regularly publishes articles on how to expose and pushback against CRT, and offers a "Critical Race Theory Legislation Tracker" to see what's happening in your state.

Toolkits for Challenging CRT

Chalkboard Review, billed as "a site of education commentary that features a diverse range of voices on all things education," has a staff that believes "intellectual diversity benefits American education and therefore seek to publish a thoughtful range of voices from teachers to advocates, scholars, and industry leaders – left, right, and center."

As such, CR has released a **"Critical Race Theory Toolkit: For Parents, Teachers, Administrators, & Everyone Else,"** which seeks to educate the public on all things CRT. The toolkit provides a brief history of CRT, its core scholars, evidence of CRT in schools, how to advocate against CRT, along with additional resources. The toolkit can be accessed on CR's website: https://thechalkboardreview.com/crt-toolkit

Christopher Rufo's "Critical Race Theory Briefing Book" is another invaluable resource for challenging CRT. The book contains definitions of CRT, key concepts and quotations, a section on "Winning the Language War," "Using Stories to Build the Argument," and documents that contain polling data and state legislation. This document can be found on Chris Rufo's website: https://christopherrufo.com/crt-briefing-book/

Critical Race Training in Education is a resource "for parents and students concerned about how Critical Race Theory, and implementation of critical race training, impacts education." Cornell Law School professor William Jacobson and his team have researched and documented critical race training in over 300 colleges and universities in the United States, and this resource allows parents and students to see if, and in what capacity, CRT is infiltrating their school.

CRTE's website (https://criticalrace.org) also "explains Critical Race Theory itself and provides resources to learn more. Additionally, it allows users to look up the steps their school has taken to mandate critical race training in different parts of the college experience, from changing academic codes of conduct to funding 'equity' projects."

New Discourses, founded by Dr. James Lindsey, is perhaps the ultimate toolkit when it comes to CRT and the battle over language and discourse.

The website (https://newdiscourses.com) includes a complete "Social Justice Encyclopedia," a section on "Grievance Studies," an incredible archive of CRT-related articles and analysis, and most importantly, a consulting service.

The Manhattan Institute recently released an issue brief titled, **"Woke Schooling: A Toolkit for Concerned Parents,"** which is an excellent resource for pushing back against CRT. The brief gives detailed information on critical pedagogy (CRT), ways to fight back, and supplies "A Critical Pedagogy Glossary," which defines terms related to CRT. It also has a section titled "What Can Parents Do?", and "Whom Can I Ask for Help?"

The toolkit can be downloaded as a PDF file on their website: https://www.manhattan-institute.org/woke-schooling-toolkit-for-concerned-parents

CRT and the Law

In addition to the "CRT Checklist" provided by **Schoolhouse Rights** (mentioned in the previous section), the following are examples of curriculum and training materials that may violate the rights of students and/or teachers, and may be subject to litigation by an attorney.[63]

- Any class or homework assignment that asks students to list their identities, and uses the labels "power/privilege." This could be a compelled speech issue, invasion of privacy, or discrimination, especially if no parental consent is given (as these assignments are surveys).

- Any curriculum material or school promotional literature promoting or endorsing the use of "Whiteness," "White supremacy," "White identity," "ally," "privilege," "dominant group," "internalized dominance," "silence is violence," "structural/systemic racism," "colorblindness," "affinity spaces," "microaggressions," "heteronormative," "BLM week," "anti-Blackness," "western nuclear family," "decentering Whiteness," or "deconstructing" anything that disparages religion or Christianity, etc. There can be legal action if any imagery or message is so offensive and racially charged that it shocks the conscience of a reasonable person. If it's pervasive enough it can result in a lawsuit under Title VI (hostile environment, racial harassment, and establishment clause).

- Any teacher training materials on diversity, equity, and inclusion (DEI), social emotional learning (SEL), anti-racism, implicit bias, culturally responsive training, equity, etc. These trainings may be grounds for litigation if participants are divided by race during training, harassed, or had their speech compelled, etc. (Title VI, hostile environment, and harassment.)

- Any pronoun policies (for teachers or students), affinity spaces, and "privilege walks" may be subject to legal action (Title VI & 14th Amendment violations, 1st Amendment chilled speech, Title IX).

---

[63] Always consult with an attorney concerning such matters.

- Any anonymous bias/microaggression reporting policy, vague speech codes for students/teachers may be grounds for litigation (1st Amendment chilled speech).

- Any instance of a school and/or district removing traditional books or classics from library for political reasons (1st Amendment).

- Participating in protests as class activities or for extra credit, or instructing students in class to raise their fists (1st Amendment).

Recommended Reading

Below is a recommended reading list containing books and articles that critique and analyze CRT and all of its related offshoots.

Books

Critical Race Theory, the New Intolerance, and Its Grip on America, Jonathan Butcher and Mike Gonzalez, *The Heritage Foundation*

Critical Race Theory Would Not Solve Racial Inequality: It Would Deepen It, Christopher Rufo, *The Heritage Foundation*

Cynical Theories: How Activist Scholarship Made Everything about Race, Gender, and Identity—and Why This Harms Everybody, by Helen Pluckrose and James Lindsey

Exploring White Fragility: Debating the Effects of Whiteness Studies on America's Schools, by Christopher Paslay.

Reinventing Racism: Why "White Fragility" is the Wrong Way to Think About Racial Inequality, by Jonathan Church

Articles

"An Economic Theory of Whiteness," *Areo Magazine*, by Jonathan Church

"Are Micro-Aggressions Really A Thing?", *The Good Men Project*, by Jonathan Church

"Dear White People: Please Do Not Read Robin DiAngelo's 'White Fragility'," *Arc Digital*, by Jonathan Church

"Diversity Training Shouldn't Be Based on Flawed Implicit Bias Research," *The Philadelphia Inquirer*, by Christopher Paslay

"How to Talk to Your Employers About Anti-Racism," *New Discourses*, by Helen Pluckrose and James Lindsay

"How 'White Fragility' Theory Turns Classrooms Into Race-Charged Power Struggles," *The Federalist*, by Jonathan Church and Christopher Paslay

"Ibram Kendi's Thesis Could Use a Lot More Rigor Part 1," *Merion West*, by Jonathan Church

"Ibram Kendi's Thesis Could Use a Lot More Rigor Part 2," *Merion West*, by Jonathan Church

"Is Whiteness Invisible to White People?", *Areo Magazine*, by Jonathan Church

"Mandatory Implicit Bias Training Is a Bad Idea," *Psychology Today*, by Lee Jussim

"Not White Fragility, Mutual Responsibility," *Patheos*, by George Yancy

"On 'White Fragility,'" by Matt Taibbi, contributing editor for *Rolling Stone*

"Psychology's Favorite Tool for Measuring Racism Isn't Up to the Job," *The Cut*, by Jesse Singal

"Robin DiAngelo's White Fragility Theory Falls Prey to Logical Fallacies," *Merion West*, by Jonathan Church

"Teaching Robin DiAngelo's 'White Fragility' Will Get You Sued," *The Federalist*, by Adam Mill

"The Creators of the Implicit Association Test Should Get Their Story Straight," *Intelligencer,* by Jesse Singal

"The Dehumanizing Condescension of White Fragility," *The Atlantic,* by John McWhorter

"The Epistemological Problem with White Fragility Theory," *Areo Magazine,* by Jonathan Church

"The False Dichotomy in Kimberle Crenshaw's Intersectionality," *Merion West,* by Jonathan Church

"The Flaws in White Fragility Theory: A Primer," *New Discourses,* by Helen Pluckrose and Jonathan Church

"The Insidious Subtext of "Systemic Racism," *The Agonist Journal,* by Jonathan Church

"The Orwellian Dystopia of Robin DiAngelo's PhD Dissertation," *Areo,* by Jonathan Church

"The Problem I Have with the Concept of White Privilege," *The Good Men Project,* by Jonathan Church

"The Problem with 'White Fragility' Theory," *Quillette,* by Jonathan Church

"The Theory of White Fragility: Scholarship or Proselytization?", *Areo Magazine,* by Jonathan Church

"What Can A Jeopardy! Episode Tell Us about White Racial Illiteracy?", *Arc Digital,* 2018, by Jonathan Church

"What To Read Instead Of 'White Fragility'," *The Federalist,* Mark Hemingway

"White Fragility Theory Is a Bullying Rhetorical Tactic," *The Agonist,* by Jonathan Church

"White Fragility Theory Mistakes Correlation for Causation," *Areo Magazine,* by Jonathan Church

"Whiteness Studies: An Insidious Ideology," *The Agonist,* by Jonathan Church

"Whiteness Studies and the Theory of White Fragility Are Based on a Logical Fallacy," *Areo Magazine,* by Jonathan Church

A Final Note to Parents

To the parents fighting against CRT, remember: ***You are not racist or bad people.*** Your instincts about Critical Race Theory are correct, and that feeling in your gut – the one that says something just isn't right in your child's school – is authentic and real. Something *isn't* right in K-12 education today, and more and more parents are waking up to this reality every day.

You are not alone. The majority of Americans oppose CRT. You may have been told otherwise, by another parent or teacher or school board member who insists you are ignorant or misinformed, that you are simply a member of some fringe group getting in the way of progress, but they have it *backwards*. You are part of a steadily growing movement of concerned parents across America, mothers and fathers of all races and political affiliations, who know in their hearts CRT is the wrong way to go.

You are on the right side of history. The pushback against CRT is an organic extension of the Civil Rights Movement, and falls directly in line with Dr. Martin Luther King Jr.'s "Dream." Those pushing CRT, who now teach that color-blindness is "racist," are the ones who have lost their way. History will expose their cynicism, polarization, and vindictiveness, and reveal that using an identity-based approach focusing on skin color – as opposed to a principle-based approach focusing on the content of character – was wrong-headed and counterproductive.

We will prevail.

We will succeed.

We will defeat CRT and bring all people together as Americans and as human beings.

About the Author

CHRISTOPHER PASLAY is a longtime Philadelphia public schoolteacher, education writer, and track coach. He's a certified Pennsylvania school counselor with an M.Ed. in multicultural education. His articles on school reform have appeared in numerous publications, including *The Philadelphia Inquirer*, *The Federalist*, *Merion West*, and *Real Clear Politics*.